My First Book about
Polar Bears

Amazing Animal Books
Children's Picture Books

By Molly Davidson

Mendon Cottage Books

JD-Biz Publishing

Download Free Books!
http://MendonCottageBooks.com

Read More Amazing Animal Books

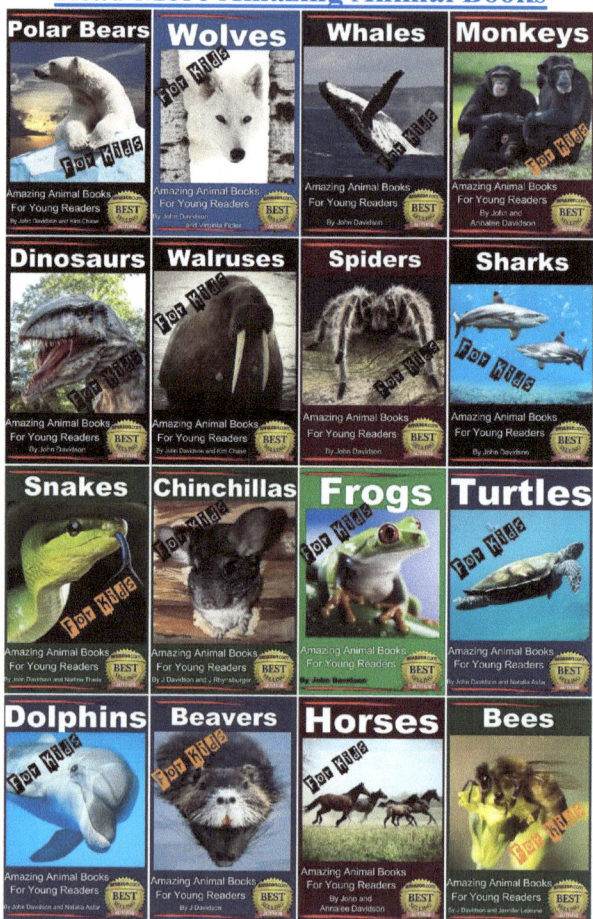

Purchase at Amazon.com

Download Free Books!
http://MendonCottageBooks.com

Table of Contents

Introduction

Have you ever wondered how a poar bear survives in the freezing cold? What they eat? Or how they talk to eat other?

Let's read and see what we can learn about these powerful bears!

About Polar Bears

Polar bears that live in the wild, live to be about 15 - 18 years old.

Polar bears are very smart, scientists believe that polar bears are as smart as apes.

A hungry polar bear was seen smashing open blocks of ice to get to the fish that were frozen inside.

Polar bears have very good eyesight, hearing, and sense of smell.

Their teeth are very sharp and spaced far apart. This helps them when they eat, and to hold onto their prey.

Polar Bears Features

A Polar Bear's fur is actually hollow and clear, not white.

After a long winter, the oil from the seals they eat makes them look yellow, but then they molt (shed) most of their fur, making them look clean and white again.

Polar Bears have black skin, that is about 4 1/2 inches thick.

A Polar Bears skin is what keeps them warm, not thier fur.

Their paws can measure 12 inches across; having thier feet be so wide helps them spread out their weight on thin ice.

They are the only bear that can swim; they use their front legs to paddle, and their back legs to steer.

Polar Bears walk very slowly, about 3 - 4 miles per hour (mph), if they have cubs, it is even slower.

If they are hunting, they can run as fast as 25 miles per hour.

Polar Bears have strong, sharp, curved, and long claws, which can be up to 2 inches long.

They use their claws to help grip the ice and for eating their prey.

What Polar Bears Do

Polar bears like to be dry and clean, if they get wet and dirty it is harder to stay warm.

In the summer, they love to swim in the water and spend time lots of time cleaning themselves.

In the winter, they clean themselves by rubbing on the snow.

A mother polar bear will lick her cubs to keep them clean, as they grow they will learn to clean themselves.

They also like to sleep, they usually sleep for about 7 - 8 hours, plus they may nap during the day.

In the spring and summer, polar bears sleep on the shore during the day, and hunt seals at night, because that's when seals are active.

The arctic has 24 hours of sun in the summer, so the polar bears don't really know when it is day or night.

They like to nap after eating, this is one way they save up energy.

How Polar Bears Talk

Polar bears talk with sounds and movements.

If they wiggle their head back and forth they want to play.

When they get angry, they let out loud growls and roars.

Polar bears charge with their heads down, ears pinned back, and sometimes making a hissing sound.

A mother bear may warn her cubs of danger with a short chuffing sound.

If something threatens her cubs she will rush towards them, warning them to stay away.

Baby Polar Bears

Before a baby polar bear is born, the mother will make a den for them.

The den can be built in snowdrifts, in a moutain, by the shore, wherever the mother thinks she can keep her cubs safe.

Baby bears are only in their mothers for about 9 weeks, and are born, usually as a set of twins, in November and December.

Newborn bears weigh about 1 pound, and are blind.

The mother and her babies do not leave the den until March or April.

The Cubs will stay with their mother for the next 2 1/2 years.

She will teach them how to hunt, clean, and protect themselves.

Where to Polar Bears Live

Polar Bears live in the far north in the Arctic where it is very cold, in places like Alaska , Greenland, Canada, Norway, and Russia.

They live on the sea ice, which is ice that has formed over the ocean.

When the sea ice starts to melt they have to head back into the shore.

Polar bears stay in an area called a home range, they are much bigger areas than compared to other bears.

They may traveled up to 600 miles to find their own home range that has enough food to substain them.

Habitat of Polar Bears

Polar bears like the cold tempertaures of the Arctic, which can be as cold as -50°F!

They build dens in the snow that help them stay out of the wind and protected when blizards come.

Some polar bears let the snow cover them like a blanket, helping to keep them insulated and warm.

During the summer, polar bears dig sleeping pits along the shoreline either in the gravel ridges, or in the sand.

Arctic Polar Bears

Polar bears only live in the Arctic around the North Pole, they don't live by the South Pole in Antarctica.

Arctic in Greek means bear, and the opposite is Antarctic, meaning without bear.

Peguins live in the Antarctic, but not in the Arctic, polar bears and penguins live on opposite poles of the Earth.

From October to February the Arctic does not see the sun, the average tempertature is -29°F.

The polar bear has lots of insulation, so it stays warm no matter how cold.

Why are the Polar Bears Endangered

Many animals that live in the cold are facing the same problem, the Earth is warming up, this is called global warming.

The problem with global warming is there is less sea ice for the polar bear to live on.

With less sea ice, polar bears have to swim farther to find ice, this can make cubs too cold and they wear out, many do not make it.

Polar bears are also threatened by poachers, pollution in the air, and less space because indutries are taking up their space.

If something doesn't change, scientists guess 66% of the polar bears will be gone by the year 2050, and all the polar bears will be gone by the year 2100.

What Polar Bears Eat

Polar bears mainly eat seals.

They wait by a seal's breathing hole in the ice, then grab them when they come up through the hole.

They will also stalk seals, they will walk very carefully to where the seal is laying, then when they are really close they charge and pounce on the seal.

A polar bear may also catch a seal while they are both swimming underwater.

Polar bears can eat up to 100 pounds of seal fat at one time.

Polar bears will eat other foods like fish, walrus, or whales, but this is only if they are really hungry.

Other Names for Polar Bears

The scientific name for a polar bear is Ursus maritimus, which means sea bear.

The Greek name for polar bear is Thalarctos, this means sea bear of the north.

The Eskimos and Inuit people the polar bear Nanuk.

Beliy medved is the Russian name, and it means white bear.

Isbjorn, meaning ice bear, is the name given to the polar bear by the people of Denmark and Norway.

In Norse poetry, the polar bears were as smart as 11 men, and had the strength of 12.

A Siberian tribe, called the Ket, call the polar bear "Gyp", which means grandfather. They also call them "Qoi", which is the word for stepfather.

Tornassuk, meaning master of the helping spirits, is the name given to the polar bear by the people of eastern Greenland.

Polar Bear Facts

Polar bears have two layers of fur, and a thick layer of fat, so they can stay warm.

Polar bears can swim for almost 100 miles at a time.

After a polar bears runs it has to be careful not to overheat.

Polar bears have a strong sense of smell.

Polar bears are the largest of all the bears.

 The boys can weigh up to 1,200 pounds, the girls about 600 pounds, and when they stand on their back legs they can be as tall as 10 feet.

Read More Amazing Animal Books

Purchase at Amazon.com

Our books are available at

1. Amazon.com
2. Barnes and Noble
3. Itunes
4. Kobo
5. Smashwords
6. Google Play Books

Download Free Books!
http://MendonCottageBooks.com

Publisher

JD-Biz Corp

P O Box 374

Mendon, Utah 84325

http://www.jd-biz.com/

Mendon Cottage Books

P O Box 374, Mendon Utah 84325

www.ingramcontent.com/pod-product-compliance
Lightning Source LLC
Chambersburg PA
CBHW050845290526
45792CB00002B/534